ZC HORSES
LEROY
THE STALLION!

Diane W. Keaster

illustrated by Debbie Page

©Copyright Sept. 2003, All Rights Reserved, ZC Horses, Diane W. Keaster, Salmon, Idaho.

No portion of this book may be reproduced in whole or in part, or stored in a retrieval system, or transmitted in any form or by any means, electronic, mechanical, photocopying, recording or otherwise, without written permission from the author.

ISBN 0-9721496-5-1

Printed in Canada

ZC HORSES LEROY THE STALLION!

To my wonderful husband Chuck who has brought a bright shining light into my life .

ZC HORSES
SERIES

Be part of them all!

Chick - The Beginning!

Chick - The Saddle Horse!

Chick - The Mom!

Luke - The First!

Barbie - The Best!

Leroy - The Stallion!

And Many More!

ZC HORSES
LEROY
THE STALLION!

INDEX

1. Ranch Chores 7
2. My Stallion 15
3. Training 23
4. Bear Valley Lake 29
5. Bob Marshall 39
6. Mill Lake 47
7. Wildlife 53
8. The Father 61
9. Tragedy Strikes 67
10. With Me 73

1

RANCH CHORES

Growing up on a ranch was wonderful. There were so many things to do. I had fun all of the time. The spry dogs and fluffy cats were my friends. They played with me whenever I wanted. Calves (baby cows) always wanted to know what I was doing. Ducks followed me around. I never got bored.

My family and I spent a lot of time together, too. Although we all worked hard, we did special things.

There was a lot of work to do, too, on a ranch. Many chores had to be done. Each season of the year housed a different chore. In the winter, cows and horses were fed hay. The hay had to be made into bales in the summer. Spring was when calves were born. Mother cows had to be watched at that time. Fall was when all the cows were brought home from their pastures. (A pasture is land where cattle graze or eat.) There was not a time throughout the year that we were not busy.

Another chore had to be done mostly in the spring and summer. It was fixing the fence around the pasture. If the fence was not in good shape, cows and calves might escape and get lost.

There are different types of fences. Some are made only out of wood. Others have wooden posts standing up with wire stretched very tightly between the posts. There may be four or five strands, or lines, of wire from the top of the post to near the bottom.

We had mostly wire fences. We always used barbed wire. It is smooth wire with small, sharp spikes along it. Once the wooden post is standing, the barbed wire is then stretched between the posts. We used a special tool called fencing pliers. These pliers cut wire and pounded staples around the wire to hold it in place. The pliers also gripped the wire to pull it good and tight. Fence stretchers pull the wire even tighter.

When I was young, I helped my brother, Bruce, fence. One pasture we fenced was the Summer Pasture. It was on a mountain called Tiger Butte. This was my favorite place to be. Beautiful wild flowers made the fields look like a quilt. There were caves at the edge of the pasture. Their walls donned writing from hundreds of years earlier.

One problem with the Summer Pasture was that it was very rocky. Spread around were small rocks and large rocks. Some were round and smooth. Others were sharp and rough. Driving across the field in the pickup was like sitting on a bouncing ball.

Bruce always drove the truck. He had the steering wheel to hold on to as we hopped across the field. I had nothing to hold onto. Once we hit a bump so hard, I flew across the cab of the pickup. I landed right on top of my brother. He was not very happy with me!

After I landed on my brother, I rode in the back of the pickup for a while. I sat contently with the

fence posts and rolls of wire. A tin bucket held the pliers and staples. All of the tools hitting together sounded like an orchestra. They played a wonderful song as I watched the fluffy clouds float through the deep-blue sky. Every so often, a cautious coyote scurried across the hillside. Sitting outside was not that bad!

Another way to fix fence is to ride horse. When I did this, I kept my pliers, staples, and anything else I needed in my saddlebag. A saddlebag is a leather bag attached to the back of the saddle.

I have wonderful memories of riding a very special horse while I was fencing.

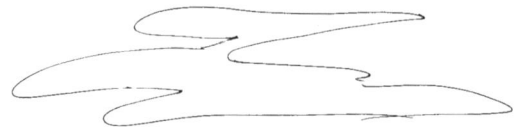

2

MY STALLION

One horse I enjoyed riding when I fixed fence was very special. His mother was one of my favorite horses. Her name was Barbie. Her coat was colored gray. Her father was also a gray-colored horse. His name was Dan. He was a beautiful stallion. A stallion is a male horse that can be a father. A gelding is a male horse that cannot be a father.

After owning Dan, I wanted to have another gray stallion. Since Barbie was gray, there would be a good chance of her foals, or babies, being gray. It would not matter what color the father was.

I had once owned a gelding that was very smooth to ride. He also was extremely cowy. That meant he naturally knew how to work cows. He enjoyed it, too. He was very smart, gentle, and good-looking. I enjoyed him so much. I wanted a baby out of his father.

The father of this gelding was 'My Leroy Brown'. He was a Quarter Horse. His shiny coat was dark brown. He looked black. He had won horse races. He also was a champion cow-cutting horse. This is a contest where very cowy horses compete. They cut, or move back and forth, just as the cow does.

My Leroy Brown was almost thirty years old. A horse, if it is taken care of, may live to be in its twenties. A twenty-five year old horse is very old. Once horses get to be about twenty, they usually are no longer ridden. I felt if I was going to have any babies from My Leroy Brown, I should do it now.

I had to wait a long, eleven months to see this special foal. Barbie was in a lush, green pasture with a small creek running through. I checked her often as she neared the time the baby was going to drop, or be born. I wondered what color the baby would be. Would it be gray, like Barbie, or brown, like its father? I had already planned if the baby was gray and a colt, or boy foal, I would keep him as my stallion.

Every time I checked on Barbie, she slowly wandered over to me. With her head low and her tummy extremely large, she stood for me to pet her. She always loved for me to show her attention. Her brown eyes always had a look of kindness.

I drove by Barbie's pasture in the middle of the day. The sun's rays were warming the land. The air was filled with freshness. I could not believe what I saw. There beside her was a beautiful, black colt. I had my new gray stallion!!

There were gray hairs through the colt's soft, furry body. A gray horse is always a dark color when it is born. Barbie was a very deep, dark red when she was born. Now her soft coat was a lighter gray, almost white. A gray horse gets lighter as it gets older.

Using both of the parents' names, I dubbed the baby 'Leroy's Bar and Dial'. From then on he was called Leroy.

Leroy had such a bright sparkle in his eyes. As soon as he was born,

I held him in my arms. He felt so velvety and warm. I could feel the muscles he already had. He did not fight me at all. He was so calm and gentle. He was very smart, too. I knew he would make a wonderful stallion.

When Leroy was young, he spent his time in the pasture with Slick. Slick was solid black. He was a year older than Leroy. They both had the same father. They ran and frolicked and bucked together. They had a lot of fun. The two of them would be deep in the pasture where I could not see them. Leaning against the rough fence post, I let out my shrill whistle. They came running at their fastest from miles away. Whether darting through the snow, mud or dust, they got to me quickly.

Leroy always was glad to see me. He was glad to see me even when the work began!

3

TRAINING

When Leroy was two years old, it was time to break him. This means he was to learn to wear a saddle and be ridden.

Leroy was about fifteen hands tall when I started riding him. Barbie was about fifteen hands tall. Leroy's father was a little bigger. Instead of a horse being measured in feet, like we are, they are measured in hands. A hand equals four inches. The horse is measured with a tape measure from its front hoof to its withers. The withers are at the bottom of the neck. It is a small area that is the highest spot where the horse's back begins. Fifteen times four is 60. A fifteen-hand horse measures 60 inches from the front hoof to the top of the withers.

Many times a young horse will be rather wild to ride the first time. Since I had put a saddle on Leroy when he was a year old, the saddle did not bother him.

Leroy's body was very muscular now. His smooth coat looked blue at this age. Even though I was ready for Leroy to jump, or even buck like his Grandmother Chick did, he did not do a thing. He acted like he had been ridden forever. Every time I rode him, he got better. He was like his father, very intelligent.

When you are breaking a colt, it is important to ride him every day. That I did. It did not matter how hot or cold the weather was. We rode every day. Even if I was tired, we still rode. Even if Leroy was tired, we rode. Sometimes in the hot sun, Leroy's neck lathered up with sweat. The smell of horse lingered on even when we were done.

Whenever I saw or smelled a

storm brewing as we rode, we rushed home. It made me think of a time when my brother, Gary, was riding his horse, Buck. He was gathering cows from a pasture. A storm started so quickly he was stuck in it. All of a sudden, a bolt of blinding lightning dropped from the sky. It struck a cow and calf. Gary rushed back home through the pelting rain. Thunder rumbled through the sky. Lightning continued to fall. He made it safely home.

The more I rode Leroy, the closer we got. I could tell he loved me. I loved him very much. He would look at me with his soft, brown eyes. The sparkle was always there. It seemed he understood every word I spoke to him. I talked to him continually when we were riding. He listened intently.

Training Leroy was fun. The most fun came later!

4

BEAR VALLEY LAKE

Part of the fun of training a horse to ride is using them. Leroy took me on many wonderful rides. Some rides were on the sagebrush-covered flat area. Most of the rides were in the tree-covered mountains.

One ride I will always cherish was a pack trip we took. To pack in means you load all of your camping gear and food onto a horse. That horse is not ridden. We rode into a beautiful mountain lake called Bear Valley Lake. Leroy got to go on the trip with his grandmother, Chick. She packed the sleeping bags and food.

It takes several hours to get to the lake. The trail is very narrow, rocky and steep. It almost made me feel like I was a snake, slithering through the trees. The scent of the pine trees wrapped around us.

At times we had to cross small, wooden bridges. Clear springs bubbled out of the ground. The water was like crystal.
Our dogs, Darby, Page and Misty,

loved to run through the trees. When they got too hot, down in the frigid creek (in Montana, creek rhymes with trick) they plopped. Once sopping wet, off they ran. I had to be careful if I got off my horse. Darby would run and jump into my arms sopping wet. The dogs smiled and wagged their tails the whole way. If we could not see them, we listened for their panting. We always knew where they were.

Chipmunks and squirrels chattered their warnings to each other. Everyone knew we were on our way! Sometimes we heard timber cracking. The hidden, majestic elk (a large member of the deer family) tried their hardest to get away before we saw them. We saw them, though. The deer did not mind us as much. They allowed us to enjoy their beauty and grace.

When the horses sensed the moose (an even bigger member of the deer family) watching, they became nervous. Most horses are quite afraid of a moose. A moose will charge a horse.

The ride to the lake was strenuous. Once there, we realized the hard work was worth it. The beauty was amazing. Walls of rock rose from three sides of the lake. Beautiful, green pine trees protected the other side. The lake sat in a bowl. This bowl was probably created from a glacier. A glacier is a huge sheet of ice that forms in the mountains. It is caused when the temperature remains below freezing. A hole is sometimes left when the glacier gradually melts and moves.

The lake housed many fish. Mostly cutthroat, rainbow and brook trout resided there. Some fish are small. Other fish are bigger. Once the horses were unsaddled, fed and content, it was time to fish! With a fishing pole in hand, to the edge of the lake we went. The fishing line danced in the air, begging the fish to bite the hook. Sometimes fish jumped out of the lake to bite at the fly on the end of the line. It would not matter if a fish did bite. It was fun watching them.

Gathering up small pieces of wood, we prepared to start a campfire. The towering trees sheltered us. Once the fire was going, our supper was prepared. The horses watched intently, wondering if they could join in. Leroy always stood quietly beside his grandmother.

When darkness fell on us, it was time to go to bed. We set up our tents and shimmied in. The smell of the doused campfire hung over us. The door to the tent had to be left open. We did not want to miss anything! It was hard to fall asleep watching the surrounding beauty. The stars twinkled through the branches of the trees. Interrupting the silence of the night was a nocturnal orchestra. A nocturnal animal is one that is active at night. The crickets, owls and coyotes were the main players in this orchestra. The horses listened calmly. It felt nice knowing I was sleeping close to Leroy.

When morning slipped over the top of the mountain, another fire was started. It was time to fry bacon and eggs. Its aroma brought all of us to life! The popping of the grease over the fire broke the silence of the morning. It stung if the grease hit my arm.

Fishing poles were active again! Leroy was glad to see me awake. He tossed a gentle whinny at me when our eyes met.

We cleaned everything up and packed it on Chick. Once the horses were saddled, we headed back home. It was hard to leave! We would be back.

Although this was a wonderful ride, there were more to come!

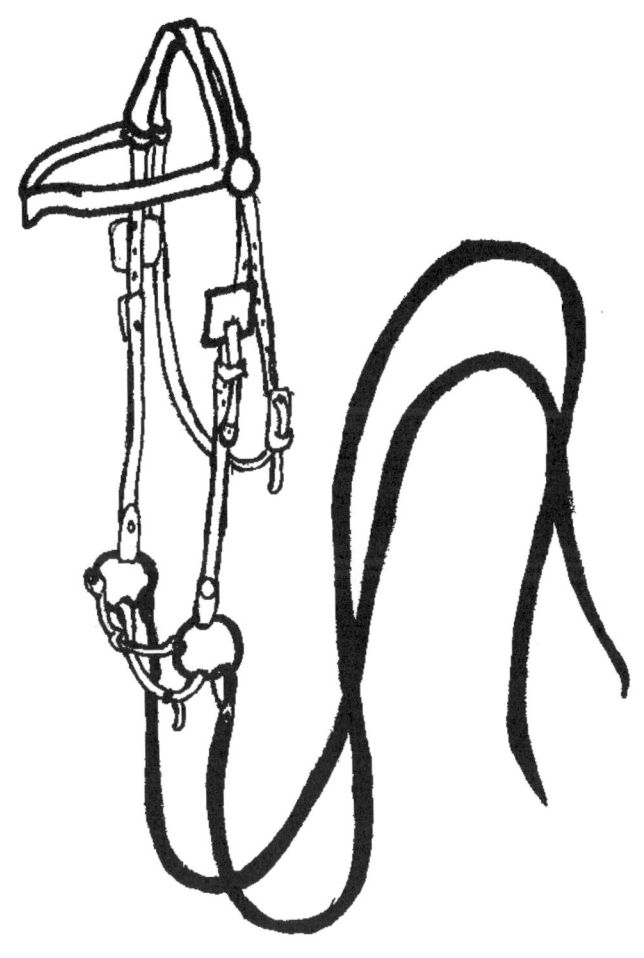

5

BOB MARSHALL

Leroy carried me many miles through the forests. Like his father, he was very smooth to ride.

Sometimes it was fun to lope, or run, through the forest. Leroy would gracefully glide over the fallen logs like he was a bird. He had what is called a rocking-chair lope. His lope was smooth and slow. Riding him when he was loping was like sitting in a rocking chair. Back and forth we went. So smoothly. So gently.

Riding Leroy reminded me of riding his mother, Barbie. She gave me many nice rides, too. One ride in particular stayed on my mind.

Every year my brothers, Gary and Steve, ride horses into the Bob Marshall Wilderness in the Rocky Mountains. A wilderness is an area of wild land where no one lives. The Bob Marshall Wilderness is in the northwest part of Montana. It is right along the Continental Divide. Rivers on the east side of the Divide flow to the Atlantic Ocean. Rivers on the west side of the Divide flow to the Pacific Ocean. The only way into the Bob Marshall Wilderness is by horseback or walking.

One year I rode into the wilderness with my brothers. We started at Swift Reservoir. A reservoir is a lake. This is against the Rocky Mountain front. It is as if the mountains form a wall against the plains. The land is flat, and then the mountains jut up. There is even an area called the Chinese Wall in this wilderness.

We had been riding for a few hours. I was leading a packhorse. His name was Gunner. His lead rope felt like sandpaper in my hands. The towering mountains wore their caps of snow. The scent of Fall was in the air. The aspen tree's leaves had turned to their showy gold and orange. The aspen's leaves quiver in the slightest breeze. The tree is quite often called a quaking aspen. The air was a bit brisk.

Grizzly bears lived where we were riding. Many ranchers in the area had problems with the gigantic bears. We were on a narrow trail. Across from us was a hillside covered with shale. Shale is a rock that is formed from hardened clay or mud. It has many thin layers that separate easily. Streaking across the shale thundered an enormous, cinnamon-colored bear. We heard rocks shattering under his feet as he thrust forward. He turned toward us never slowing down. His fur flowed like the waves of an ocean as he loped away. Every muscle in his body moved as he dashed from us.

We were all quiet for a while. The bear was very close. The horses did not even know what to do! Barbie stood calmly the whole time. I think she was too scared to move.

My brothers were going to camp in the wilderness for about a week. I was riding right back out. Leaving my brothers and thinking about the bear was tough! Along the trail on the way back, there were signs of the bear. We saw where he had been eating. His gigantic footprints were in the middle of the trail. Both Barbie and I kept a close watch!

I soon learned what Leroy would do in a bad situation!

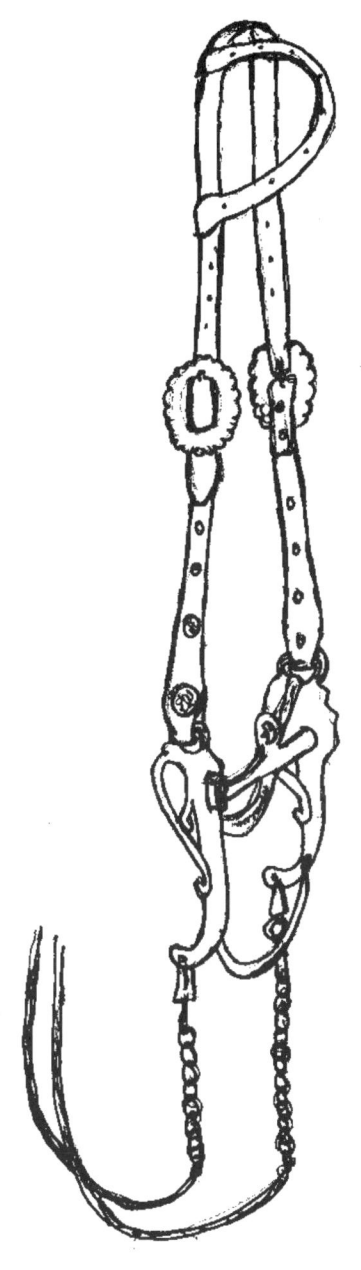

6

MILL LAKE

Another special ride was riding into Mill Lake. The lake was at the top of a mountain behind where we lived. What made this ride so special was that Page was just a puppy.

Page went with us. She was so small, she had to ride in a bag hanging from the saddle horn, the front part of the saddle. Page was black with brown around her legs and nose. She had a little white down her chest. The very tip of her tail was white.

Darby and Misty went on the ride, too.

It was early summer when we rode into the lake. The mountain snow was just melting. When the weather starts warming up, the snow at the top of the mountains starts its journey downward. Once the melted snow gets to the bottom, the creeks and rivers start raging.

To get to the lake, we had to follow a trail winding through the pine trees. The sun seemed to follow us as we rambled in and out of the trees.

As we were getting close to Mill Creek, we heard a tremendous roar. It was like thunder rolling down the mountain. When the trail was beside the creek, we saw what we heard. The mountain had let loose of its melting snow. The creek was charging down the mountain. Looking at it made you think it was coming right over you. Leroy did not know what to think. He stood with his hairy ears pointing straight up and forward.

The farther up the mountain we got the colder the air felt. Small spots of snow appeared. Darby loved the cold snow. He ran to it and jumped. Flat on his stomach he landed. He twisted around the icy bath, filling his long, white coat with it.

The snow kept getting deeper and deeper the farther we went. The ice-cold torrent was still raging. Leroy trudged through the knee-deep snow. He wondered if I was making him do the right thing. The cold snow touched Leroy's belly. We could not go on. Sadly, we turned back.

We did not complete our trek to Mill Lake that day. Later on we did. The effort to get there was worth it. The lake rested in a bowl. It was beautiful. Fish glided through the crystal-clear water.

Although the land was beautiful, there was more to enjoy from the back of Leroy!

7

WILDLIFE

Leroy allowed me to see more than the gorgeous scenery. He enabled me to see all creation. When you are on the back of a horse, wildlife is not as spooked. It is as if animals have a sense about them that lets them know they are safe. Riding a horse I observed deer, elk, moose, antelope, and mountain goat. I enjoyed mountain sheep, coyotes, wolves, eagles and so many more.

A ride when I saw much wildlife was one I took on Leroy's mom, Barbie. It was a ride to the top of Slategoat Mountain. The top of the mountain was close to 9000 feet above sea level. It was along the Rocky Mountain front, right at the Continental Divide. The small town we went through to start the ride was Augusta, Montana. Augusta admires the mountains touching what seems to be the top of the blue sky.

The ride to the top of Slategoat started by winding through fresh smelling pine trees. The trees were so thick, looking straight up was the only way you saw anything. I gazed at the marshmallow-type clouds floating through the deep blue sky. I watched as the birds far above me dotted the clouds. I imagined their shrill calls dropping to my ears.

All of a sudden the green trees vanished. A forest fire had ravaged the area the previous year. Big, black toothpicks are all that stood. Without the thick branches on the trees, you saw everything around you. A bull elk, his massive antlers looking like branches, thought he was hiding. He was easily seen.

Riding through the dormant trees,

there was total silence. Sometimes though, the silence was broken. When a slight breeze blew, a lifeless tree would creak as if in pain. Our nostrils filled with the stench of burnt wood. Both Barbie and I had an eerie feeling riding through the burn area. It had a beauty of its own.

Every so often I slid my hand down Barbie's smooth neck. This comforted her.

When we left the charcoaled trees, there was nothing. We had ridden so far up on the mountain, we were beyond what is called the tree line. Trees and plants can no longer grow any higher than this area. All that was holding us was shale. Looking straight up, we saw the top of Slategoat Mountain.

The trail zigzagged up to the peak. It seemed we could never get there. Once there, the view was awesome. We could see forever. There was only enough room at the top for maybe two or three horses. We felt like a crown atop the mountain. From our vantage point, we saw the Chinese Wall. Watching a majestic bald eagle soar by, I knew we could see whatever he was seeing. Down below us, in the black sticks, the exalted bull elk watched us. Through the full pine trees, deer quietly browsed, or nibbled on the trees. It was as if we were sneaking into their sacred abode.

A frosty breeze stung our cheeks. The beauty warmed us.
Leroy, like his mom, showed me peace and serenity in the land and wildlife. He also showed me it in another way!

8

THE FATHER

Another way Leroy showed me peace and serenity was by letting me see his children grow. Leroy himself grew to be a beautiful, magnificent stallion. It was a thrill having his grandmother Chick as a baby. Then I watched his mom, Barbie, grow from a baby. I cherished watching him grow. Then his own children.

When Leroy was two years old, it was time for him to become a father. He was able to run out in a large pasture with the mares, or female horses. Even though he was running with all of these mares, he always came racing to me when he heard my shrill whistle. He always had that same bright twinkle in his eyes.

When we needed to go for a ride, he stood quietly for me to throw the saddle on his back. He never minded leaving his brood. He loved going into the hills and mountains for a ride.

When the mares had their babies by their side, Leroy watched over them. He took care not to allow them to be hurt. When the babies were his own children, it seemed he looked at them differently. He always had a different sort of whinny for them.

It was the same with his mother, Barbie. When they saw each other, the look about them was different. They talked to each other differently.

So it was with Barbie and her mom, Chick. Time might have gone by when they did not see each other. When they did, they sent out a gentle greeting.

It seems no matter whether it is an animal or a person involved, a parent and their child always have that bond. It never goes away. No matter how long they are apart. No matter how far they are apart. Their love for each other never ends. Neither parent nor child will forget the closeness they had when the child was young.

Leroy had many children. Two very special fillies, young girl horses, were Classy and Belle. They were two years apart in age. Nellie was their mother. They look very much like their father, Leroy. When I am riding them, I am reminded of Leroy. Just like when I rode Leroy, I was reminded of his mom.

I never could have imagined that the happy times with Leroy were soon to end.

9

TRAGEDY STRIKES

Leroy could only be with the brood mares, (a mare kept for having foals) for a short time. The foal is born a little over eleven months after the stallion has been with the foal's mother. The best time for a foal to be born is between February and June. This way, the foal can be grown enough to withstand the harshness of winter. If they are born during winter their delicate ears may freeze.

Leroy was spending winter in an open pasture with some bulls. A bull is the male of the cattle family. This pasture was where he was born. He had rarely stayed anywhere else. The small creek was frozen now.

Leroy was being fed well. It was not a very severe winter. A thin layer of crusty snow carpeted the ground. I checked on him often to make sure he was okay.

Leroy happened to be near a corral as I was passing one day. I hollered out a happy hello to him as usual. I could always tell he was pleased I was there. He was starting to turn a lighter gray, now. His soft coat was still quite dark, though.

The next time I went to check on Leroy, I only saw the bulls. I whistled and whistled. He did not come. I whistled again, louder than I ever had. He still did not come. The bulls watched me, like they wanted to tell me something.

I searched the pasture. Leroy was nowhere to be found. I thought he might be hurt. There was no blood on the cold, crusty snow. There was no sign of distress. Just his footprints molded in the floor of ice.

I could not imagine what had happened. I was very distraught. The next day I hunted and hunted for him. There was not a piece of land within miles I did not check. Still he was nowhere. Leroy was gone.

I finally had to admit to myself that Leroy had been stolen. My

heart was empty. There was nothing I could do. He was so friendly. Anyone could catch him and they did.

No matter where I go in my travels I search for Leroy. I know Barbie looks for him, too. He would be quite light in color now. I will never give up finding him.

10

WITH ME

Leroy gave me so much joy. He helped me be in the midst of the beautiful mountains. He allowed me to view the majestic animals. He became a wonderful friend.

The most joy Leroy gave me was watching his children grow to be fantastic horses. I was able to hold many of his babies. Leroy's two daughters, Classy and Belle, are bringing me as much joy as Leroy did. Belle was the last of Leroy's children.

Seeing Chick, Barbie and Leroy in his children warms my heart. By riding Classy and Belle, all of my wonderful memories of Leroy fill my mind. When on Belle, I close my eyes. I glide my hand down her warm neck. It is as if I am riding Leroy again.

Although Leroy is gone from his home, I know he is making someone a wonderful horse. He could be nothing but wonderful! I am sure he is happy.

Leroy has never left my heart.
That is where he will always be.

ZC HORSES SERIES

Now that you have learned Leroy's story, meet Chick's third baby, Goldie! See how beautiful she is. Wait till you see what color she is! Hear how wise she is. Learn how she works with cows. You will adore Goldie after reading the seventh wonderful book in the **ZC HORSES** series, *"Goldie-The-Wise"*.
Be sure to be there to greet her!!

ZC HORSES SERIES #7

Goldie-The-Wise!

by Diane W. Keaster

Coming Spring 2004

To My Reader:

I was born and raised on a ranch near a little town called Belt, Montana. After receiving my B.S. in Business Education from Montana State University, I taught high school business. I then moved on to other facets of employment.

The whole time, I was team roping and raising, breaking and training horses. The profession I fell into by mistake was trading horses. Throughout my life, I have handled hundreds of horses, all which have a story of their own.

My sons, Cole and Augustus, loved reading stories about horses when they were small and I loved reading the stories to them. That is why I am writing these books. I want to tell the stories of the creatures I love to the children I love.

My husband, Chuck, and I live in beautiful Salmon, Idaho with Page, George (the bird), Belle, Classy and Barbie.

I thank Jehovah our Creator for giving us such a wonderful, beautiful animal!

Enjoy the stories!

Order Form
ZC HORSES SERIES

Don't miss out on any part of the lives of Chick and her many babies and friends! Experience all of the rides, joys and sorrows. Don't be left out!

___ Chick-The Beginning! (Spring 2001) $6.95
___ Chick-The Saddle Horse! (Summer 2001) $6.95
___ Chick-The Mom! (March 2002) $6.95
___ Luke-The First! (July 2002) $6.95
___ Barbie-The Best! (Oct. 2002) $6.95
___ Leroy-The Stallion (September 2003) $6.95
___ Goldie-The Smart! (Summer 2004) $6.95
___ Chickadee-The Traveler (March 2004) $6.95

UPCOMING TITLES

Tawny-The Beauty!	Sonny-The Spectacular!
Onie-The Roanie!	Belle-The Sweetie!
Classy-The Special!	Lily-The Pretty Paint!
Black Jack-The Great!	Darby-The Dog!
Slick-The Friend!	Apple-The Joy!

Also read about Cider, Buck, Nellie, Junie, Eagle, Smokey, Sarge, Tex, Radar and many more!

ZC HORSES SERIES, 701 S. St. Chas., Salmon, ID 83467
(208) 756-3757 or zchorses@hotmail.com
www.salmoninternet.com/zchorses

Please send me the books I have checked above. I am enclosing US $____(please add $2/bk to cover shipping and handling). Send check or money order, please.

NAME _____

ADDRESS _____

CITY/STATE/ZIP_____

PHONE (OPTIONAL)_____
Please allow four to six weeks for delivery. Shipping prices good in U.S. only. Prices subject to change.